Baby's Got the Blues

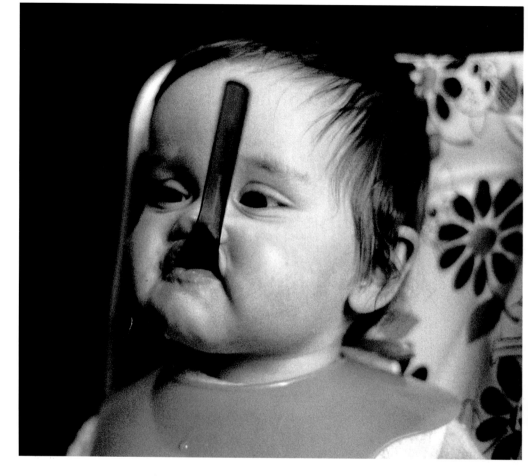

Gareth Jones

Baby's Got the Blues

Life's not always a bed of roses.

There are days when you feel a bit out of place...

...or
just
a
bit
rubbish.

Philosophy can cause headaches.

There are risks, and then there are risks.

Accept
that from
time to
time you
will say
the wrong
thing to
the wrong
person.

When
put on
the spot,
deny
everything.

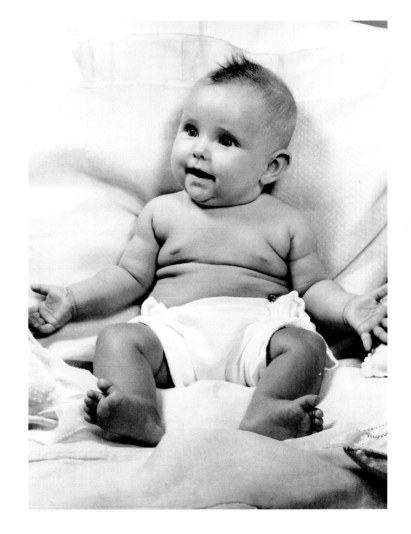

Not everything's fair in love and war.

It always seems like a good idea at the the time.

Don't
act
like a
princess.

You can
love yourself
that bit
too much.

Envy is the root of all evil.

There can be concrete reasons for it, though.

A little cheek is
acceptable...

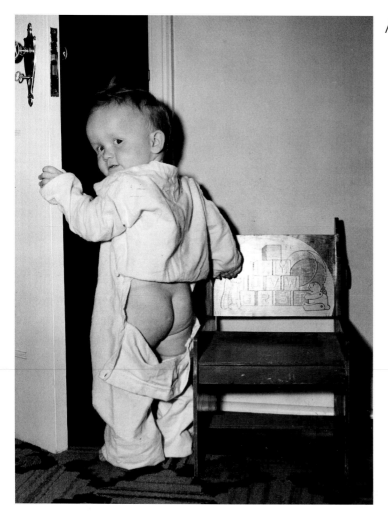

...but some people take it too far.

Youth is
wasted on
the young.

A caged bird is a terrible thing.

Have a whale of a time, but not at the expense of others.

There is never
a taxi around
when you
need one.

Brace yourself for the worst.

Love hurts.

Gifts can come from the strangest places.

Sometimes even a mascot gets an orange at half-time.

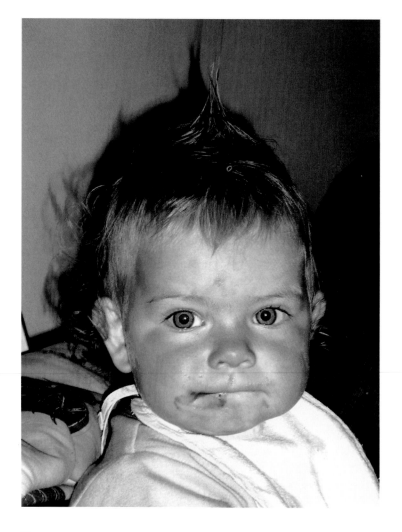

Today's cool hairstyle is tomorrow's bad hair day.

Fashion comes and goes with the seasons.

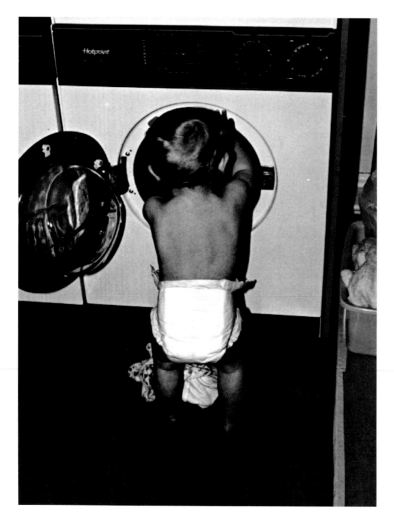

Along with black holes, odd socks are a phenomenon that may never be fully explained.

Camouflage
is best left to
the armed
forces.

While there is a good argument for the criminal
mind being nurture over nature...

...dictators
are born,
not made.

When forced into a corner, try to look tough and hope for the best.

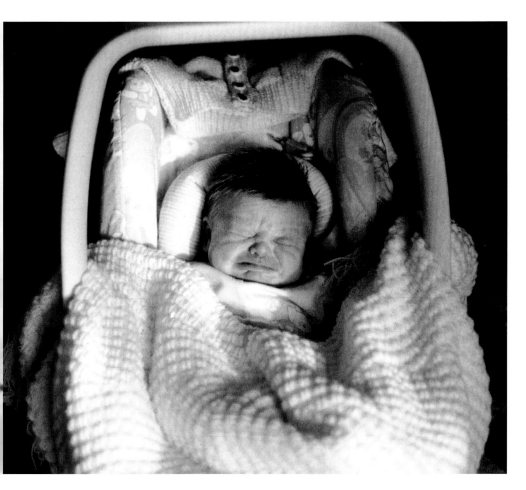

What makes a Monday morning even worse is
when you thought it was Sunday.

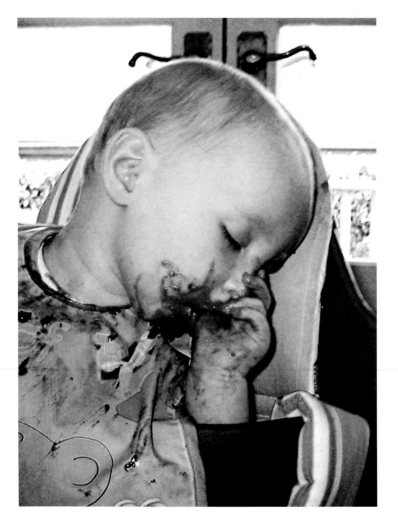

Sucking
your thumb
can all too
easily end
in tragedy.

And who knows where tragedy will lead?

Investments will go down as well as up.

Keep your friends close and your enemies closer.

Sometimes there's too much month
left at the end of your money.

If you're tired of tearing your hair out,
find a suitable victim.

41

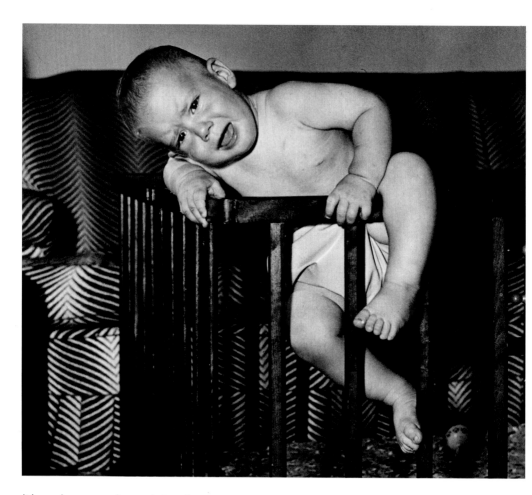

It's always best to try…

...even if you fall flat on your face.

Ploughing your own furrow is no easy task.

Character
building
generally
involves a
certain
amount of
pain.

When you try to make a splash,
sometimes only you get wet.

But if you're not paying for the water
or the bath foam, who cares?

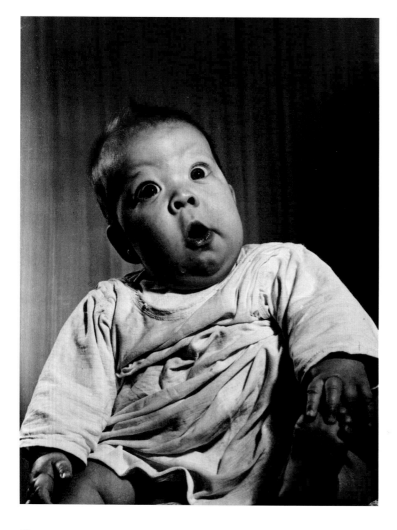

Modelling isn't
for everyone.

Package holidays just get cheaper and cheaper.

It seems everyone has a degree these days.

Bosses are
there to
be hated.

Someone else
will always get
the cream…

...then rub your face in their good fortune.

Some people just love the sound of their own voice.

Someone always gets it in the face – just make sure it isn't you.

Your route
to the top
may only
lead as far
as the attic.

Being top of
the pile can
be a daunting
prospect.

Before you take to the driving seat, make sure you know what's round the corner.

Who knows where a pub crawl will end?

You can't always fill your predecessor's boots.

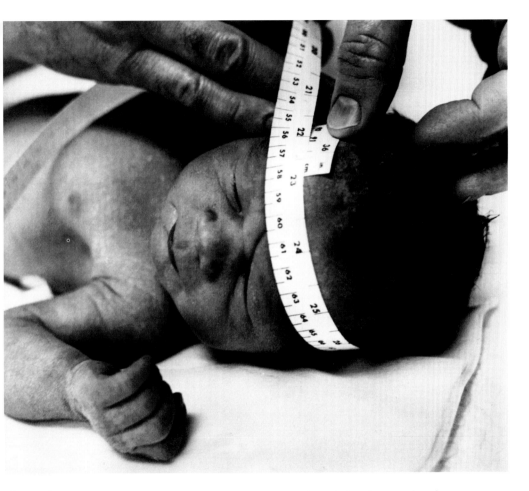

Just because someone says you're big-headed,
it doesn't mean that it's true.

61

The tea
break is the
cornerstone of
industry.

Who says it should be work, work, work, anyway?

As a rule, your pet should always be smaller than you.

There are
fewer risks
associated
with towel-
drying your
hair.

Being dish
of the day can
be more of
a curse than
a blessing.

When in
the soup,
bluff your
way out
of it.

There are those who will bet on anything.

No matter what the forecast is,
it always rains at Wimbledon.

Be at one
with nature...

...but don't feed the animals.

A hug can soften up even the toughest of customers.

A smile can brighten up the most miserable of days.

The very thought of housework can be exhausting.

The knowledge that domestic chores are easier than they were a century ago is little consolation.

One man's kitchen is another man's bombsite.

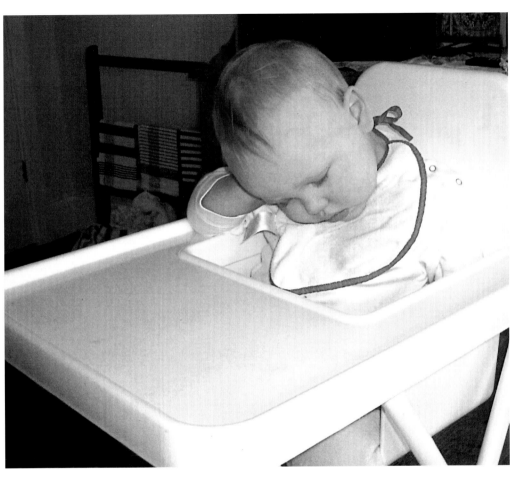

Fast food just isn't fast enough these days.

Always provide dinner guests
with a plate at the very least.

Food is always welcome too.

A high-fibre diet isn't all it's cracked up to be.

You only
need to
drink two
litres
of water
a day.

With a little food and love, you can really bloom…

...but
beware of
GM crops.

Buying in bulk is often a false economy.

Remember that there are always
people worse off than you.

Working around an obstacle usually yields better results than meeting it head on.

U-turns are occasionally necessary.

Make an effort when fancy dress is required or don't bother at all.

No matter
how much
you try to
convince
yourself
otherwise,
a wig always
looks like
a wig.

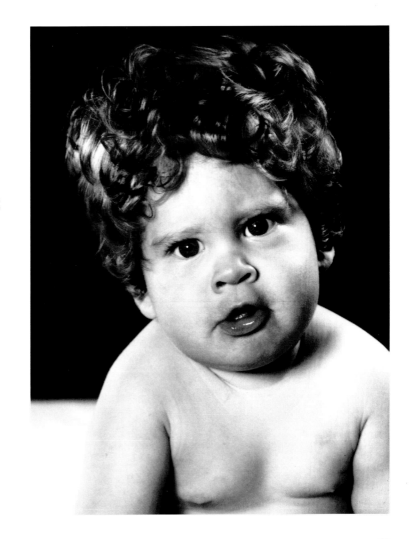

Stay cool when things are heating up around you.

Have fun
(or at least
pretend to).

Whatever you do, don't forget to turn the gas off.

Pictures

Aaron Thynne: page 92
Adriana Williams: page 29
Alan Marshall: page 37
Alex Lattes: page 82
Alfred Parker: pages 20; 31
Carolyn James: 24; 30; 73
Chris Ward: page 47
Danny Watts: page 75
Darren Gee: pages 36; 83
David Woodruffe: front cover; pages 2; 44; 54; 59; 69; 79; 96
Dorothea Grimberg: page 28
Garvin Brown: pages 41; 72
Getty Images: pages 5–19; 21–23; 25–26; 32–33; 38–40; 42–43; 46; 48–53; 60–61; 63–65; 68; 70–71; 74; 76; 81; 84–85; 87; 89
Jayne Gee: page 58
Kathleen Higgins: pages 35; 77
Lisa Wallis: pages 86; 91
Mark Reid: page 45
Martin Copley: pages 56–57; 62; 66–67; 80
Roger Blagg: pages 78; 90
Tom Kassel: pages 55; 88
Tove Liljekvist: page 27
Violaine Higueras: page 34

Dedication
To my parents for teaching me my nappy from my rattle, and for helping me realise my inner baby.

Author
Gareth Jones has often been described by friends and acquaintances as an "overgrown baby", a "toddler in a man's body" and "immature". Instead of viewing such comments in a negative way, he feels we should all learn to love and listen to our inner baby. The author of the New Holland title "Shed Men", Gareth lives and works in London.

Acknowledgements
A big thanks goes to the following people:
Everyone who took the time to hunt through their photo albums to supply us with baby photographs; Getty Images for all of the other images; Rosemary Wilkinson, Steffanie Brown and Clare Sayer for constructive criticism, suggestions and support (and for allowing me to throw temper tantrums, spit my dummy and chuck my toys out of the pram at various stages throughout the editorial process); Paul Wright for drawing the potential out of the pictures and making the best of the captions; the baby-friendly Terry Shaughnessy for all his inevitable meddling; Yvonne Thynne and Catherine Holmes for all their sterling work in publicity; Candice Nichols, Carolyn Streek and Claire Eastham for their generous feedback; and Hannah for everything.

First published in 2005 by
New Holland Publishers (UK) Ltd
London • Cape Town • Sydney • Auckland
www.newhollandpublishers.com

Garfield House
86–88 Edgware Road
London W2 2EA
United Kingdom

80 McKenzie Street
Cape Town 8001
South Africa

14 Aquatic Drive
Frenchs Forest
NSW 2086
Australia

218 Lake Road
Northcote, Auckland
New Zealand

1 3 5 7 9 10 8 6 4 2

ISBN 1 84330 983 1

Senior Editor: Steffanie Brown
Editorial Direction: Rosemary Wilkinson
Production Controller: Hazel Kirkman
Designer: Paul Wright @ Cube

Reproduction by Modern Age Repro House Ltd, Hong Kong
Printed and bound by Tien Wah Press, Malaysia.